W9-CKI-335

Dear Michelle

  Happy Grandparenting —
when the Time comes. —
          fondly
        Joyce French

Dear Michele —
  Keep sharing
your wisdom, your humor
and your hugs!
          Love —
        Marie Annwn

Michelle !
Best wishes in
all your creative
endeavors
    Mary M Branch

Grandma Needs A Nap !

Grandma Needs A Nap!

Written by
Marie Z. Amoruso & Joyce N. French

Illustrated by
Mary N. Branch

Grandma Press

Pleasantville, New York

Grandma Needs a Nap!
©Grandma Press 2012

All rights reserved. No part of this book may be reproduced or transmitted in any form or by any means—electronic or mechanical, including photocopying, recording or by any other retrieval or storage system without the written permission of the publisher.

Published by

Grandma Press
463 Old Sleepy Hollow Rd.
Pocantico Hills
Pleasantville, NY 10570

Text: Marie Z. Amoruso and Joyce N. French
Illustrations: Marie N. Branch
Cover and Interior Layout: Nick Zelinger, NZ Graphics
Technical Editor for Book and DVD: Michelle Ambruz, MAMBRUZ Post

ISBN: 978-0-9854396-0-6

LCCN: 2012937276

First Edition

Printed in China through Four Colour Print Group, Louisville, Kentucky

Production Date: June, 2012
Plant & Location: Printed by Everbest Printing (Guangzhou, China), Co. Ltd
Job / Batch #: 108171

We dedicate this book to

all the grandparents and caregivers,
who lovingly share their time
with our children.

"Thank you Mum!"

Yes, we know you are "Mum"
And you love what you do
But in spite of that fact
We are indebted to you
For the time that you spend
With our little treasures
Does more than provide you with
A grandmother's pleasures
These two little cherubs not only play
But thoroughly enjoy their "learning day"
As you spin stories galore
Create games and more
And all the while teach them
What life has in store
Letters, shapes, numbers and words
Ants, chipmunks, spiders and birds
All join in the fray
To make a most "wonder full" day
Thank you, oh thank you
For sharing your love, your wisdom, your humor
And, above all, your hugs!

Sreelekha Chakrabarty Amoruso

It's "Grandma's Day!"

We're awake,

waiting,

waiting.

"Grandma's Day" is always filled with

Surprises!

Fun!

Games!

Music!

Magic!

Grandma bounds in and scoops us up!

"Let's pretend we're Peter Pan!"

she says like a fairy godmother

waving a magic wand.

"I'm Peter Pan!" says Andy.

"I'm dressed!" says Ana,

"and

I'm

flying

straight on down

to breakfast!"

"Let's pretend we're in the jungle!"

Grandma says like a fairy godmother waving a magic wand.

"I'm a lion!"
says Ana.

"I'm a tiger!"
says Andy.

"Grrr," we devour our breakfast.

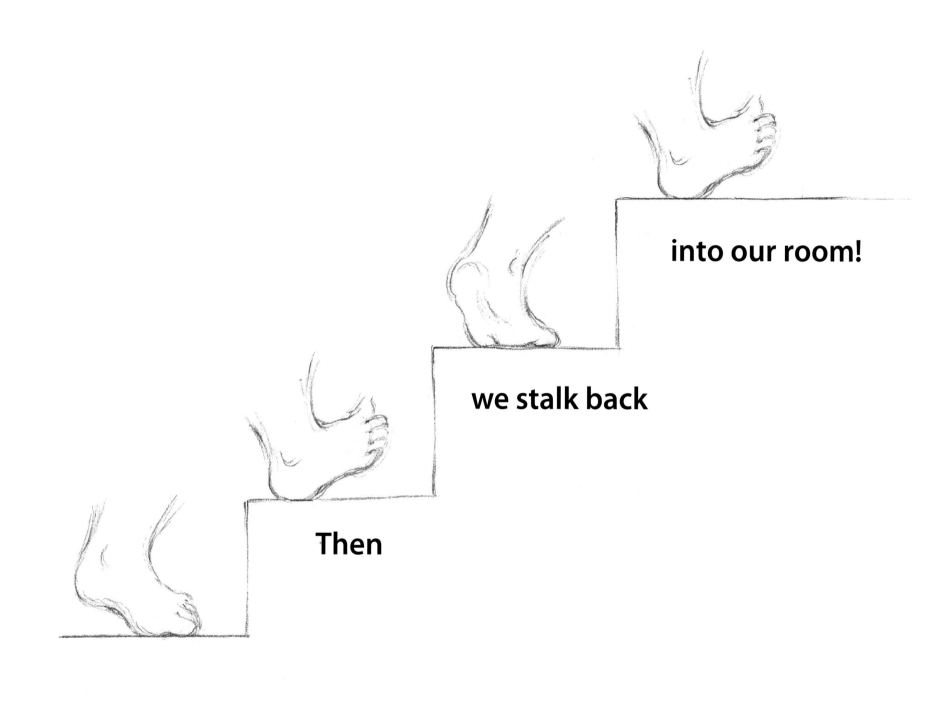

On "Grandma's Day" we do puzzles,

build with blocks,

and dance our way to foreign lands.

Grandma laughs and laughs!

Soon we climb up Mt. Sofa. Grandma reads us very special books.

We melt into her love.

We are warm and safe.

Grandma yawns, "I'm so tired. I need a nap!"

"We'll rest with you, too! But we're not going to sleep!"

We hop into our beds. She hums a soft tune.

On "Grandma's Day" before we know it...

ZZ ZZ ZZ ZZ zz.

It's "Grandma's Day!"   "Grandma, Grandma, we're awake!"

Grandma bounds in raring to go. "Ana, Andy, did you nap, too?"

"Let's pretend!" she says
    like a fairy godmother waving a magic wand.

"I'm Peter Pan!"
    says Andy.

"I'm flying!"
says Ana.

"I'm hungry!"

"Fly straight on down to the kitchen!"

On "Grandma's Day" we are chefs!
"Real chefs have snacks to make," she says.

"I am a chef!" says Ana.

"My apron and
chef's hat are on!"

"Me, too!"
says Andy.

"I want to make our snack!"

"Me too!"

Grandma says, "What color will our snack be?

What's the color of the week?"

"That's our color today!"

"I know my colors because I eat them!"

"I want to stir!"
says Ana.

"No me!" says Andy.

"WHOOPS!"...

"Some got on me."

"More got on the floor!!"

Grandma laughs, "You know your colors because you wear them!"

"I'll help clean-up!" says Ana.   "Me too!" says Andy.

"We'll make more."

Soon after, very hungry chefs eat lunch quickly.

Suddenly, Grandma's voice like a trumpet blasts, "It's 'Grandma's Day'.

Time to explore outdoors!

March!

March!

March!"

"What do we need on our feet?"

"Shoes?"

"Sneakers?"

"Boots?"

Soon we stop under a dogwood tree. Grandma reads some very special books.

We melt into her love.

We feel warm and safe.

We march back into the house, straight on to the kitchen.

"Let's pretend." She waves her magic wand!

We put on our Peter Pan Indian costumes.

We cut the red gelatin into shapes.

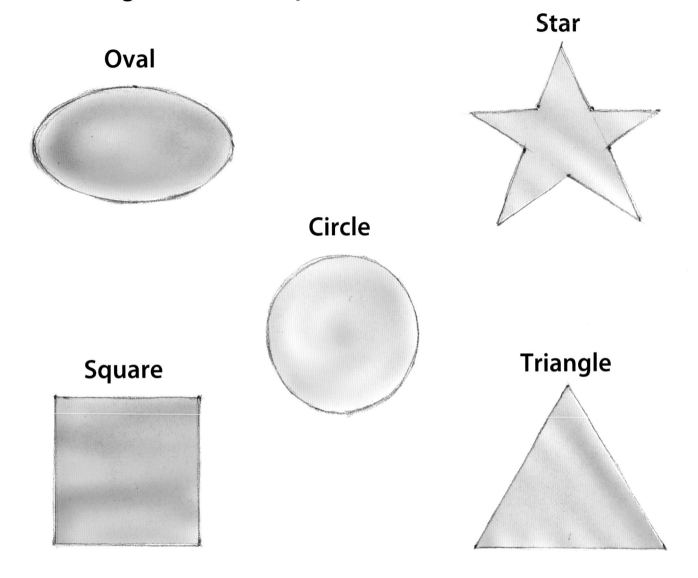

Oval

Star

Circle

Square

Triangle

"I know a square because I eat it!"

"I know a triangle because I eat it!"

We eat our red gelatin shapes in front of the T.V.
as we return to make believe land.

Wendy, Peter Pan,
Tinkerbell, and Captain Hook
appear on the screen.

We sing and dance!

Before we know it, Peter Pan is over.

We waltz into the kitchen like Wendy.

We chant "one-two-three, one-two-three."

We eat our yummy dinner.

Even clean-up is fun with Grandma.

After a warm bath with bubbles and lots of toys,

we put on our soft nighty and pajamas.

Soon we climb up Mt. Sofa. Grandma reads us some very special books.

We melt into her love.

We are warm and safe.

Grandma yawns, "I'm so tired. I need to sleep."

"We'll rest with you, too! But, we are not going to sleep!"

We flop into our beds. She hums a soft tune.

On "Grandma's Day" before we know it...

"Grandma's Day" is a day of sunshine,

surprises,

fun,

games,

music,

and magic

wrapped up in **LOVE.**

Epilogue

So many years have gone by. We are parents now, doing what she did.
Yet we still find time to see our 'Grandma'. After lunch, we read her some very special books.
We recall melting into her love, feeling warm and safe.
"Oh!" Grandma yawns. "I am so tired. I need a nap."
We pray a soft prayer. Soon she gets into her bed.
We recall her humming a soft tune,
and before we know it, she's asleep.

Yes, Grandma needs a nap and now she closes her eyes and rests, knowing we'll return each "Grandma's Day"
bringing sunshine, surprises, fun, games, music and magic wrapped in **LOVE.**

Grandma's Ideas & Hints

Outdoor Activities and Trips

such as Walks, Parks, Zoos, Botanical Gardens, Natural History and Art Museums, Historical Locations

Keep it short and make it fun!

- **Plan** short outdoor and indoor trips (stay no longer than 45-90 minutes). There will always be another day.
- Have a definite **Focus** in mind, such as:
    - ✔ one or two exhibits only, or children's zoo only
    - ✔ set out an activity plan, such as swings, slide, or balance beam
    - ✔ copy the colors seen in paintings such as Renoir, Matisse, Picasso, etc.
    - ✔ stop under a tree or on the seashore and read a short book, such as *The Hungry Caterpillar, One Fish Two Fish,* or *Brown Bear, Brown Bear*
    - ✔ find objects that are in the color or shape of the week; discover new shapes
    - ✔ draw in the sand, dirt, or with chalk on pavement, etc.
    - ✔ find leaves, flowers, rocks, shells, bugs, etc.
    - ✔ name trees, bushes, shrubs in our environment
    - ✔ see birds, animals (squirrels, etc.) in our environment
    - ✔ choose a letter in our name and find other objects that begin with that letter

- **Enjoy** the activity!
- **Follow up** by taking what is found/discovered and doing something with it, such as paste leaves onto sheets of paper, find pictures in books that match the birds seen, read a story or see a video about what you've discovered.

Recipe for Gelatin Jiggles

Ingredients: Large box of Gelatin

- **Measure** out half of the usual amount of water,
  bring it to a **Boil** and slowly add it to the gelatin
- **Stir** until all the gelatin is dissolved
- **Pour** into a brownie pan and **Chill**
- **Cut** into interesting shapes and **Enjoy** eating!

Music

Children's songs easily found on the internet and in the public library

There are many fantastic commercial CDs that focus upon early childhood, actually teach motion, and incorporate games, such as:

- Georgiana Stewart's *Choo Choo to the Zoo, Rhythm Stick Rock, Moving with Mozart, Bean Bag Activities and Coordination Skills, Circle Time Activities* [Kimbo Records in New Jersey]
- Disney CDs such as *Fantasia, Snow White, Cinderella, Lion King*, etc.
- Musicals/operas, such as Mary Martin's or Kathy Rigby's *Peter Pan*, Humberdink's *Hansel and Gretel*

Other Activities:

Card games, chalk-on-pavement drawing, games that support a theme, matching numbers, colors of the week

Commercial games (the internet or toy store can help select those that are age-appropriate)

Games/activities grandparents enjoyed as youngsters

Websites

There are many, such as *www.grandparents.com, www.fambooks.com, www.apples4theteacher.com*

Other Resources:

Public Library, Book Stores

Acknowledgments

We want to express our gratitude
to the teaching, administrative, and technical staff of

Media Arts Lab

The Jacob Burns Film Center

in Pleasantville, NY

for their support and guidance
while making the video edition of
Grandma Needs a Nap

special thanks to

Anne Marie Santoro, Faculty
Brady Shoemaker, Faculty
Yolanda Pividal, Faculty
Michelle Ambruz, Technical Editor
Emily Keating, Director of Education
Ann MacDonald, Registrar
Thom O'Connor, Director of Technology

With my grateful appreciation *per cent'anni*,
Marie Amoruso

Illustrator

Mary N. Branch

Mary N. Branch graduated with a degree in Art History from Duke University and did post-graduate studies at the Art Students League of New York while working at the Frick Museum. Her art has been exhibited at galleries such as the Institute of Contemporary Art in Boston and the Art Students League of New York, and she has won awards from various art societies for her oils, prints, pastels, and drawings.

Mary's landscape, still life, and portrait works have been influenced by the art of Mary Cassatt, Edgar Degas, and Alice Neel. Her goal is to capture on canvas the attitude and personality of the individual sitter in a fresh and contemporary way.

She is a member of the National League of American Pen Women.

Authors

Marie Z. Amoruso

Dr. Marie Zuzzolo Amoruso is an educator/author whose 50-year career includes work as a public school teacher, clinician, researcher, presenter, literary consultant to various school districts, and adjunct professor of education and psychology at Manhattanville College and Teachers College Columbia University. Her unique work brings parents into effective partnerships with teachers in public schools and was recently cited in Brassard & Boehm's *Preschool Assessment* (Guilford Press).

Dr. Amoruso holds a Doctorate in Psychology and Education with a concentration in Reading from Teachers College Columbia University, a Masters of Professional Studies in Reading and Special Education from Manhattanville College, and a Baccalaureate from Hunter College.

She lives in Pocantico Hills, NY with her husband of 50 years Don Amoruso. They have three children: Donna-Marie A. Lasco, a teacher; Donald J. Amoruso, Jr., owner of a software design engineering company; and Michael J. Amoruso, Esq., a nationally renowned elder law and estate planning attorney. She has eight magnificent grandchildren.

Joyce N. French

Joyce N. French received her doctorate from Columbia University and has been a classroom teacher, an elementary school administrator, and a college professor. She has taught all levels from first grade to graduate school and adult literacy. She worked as Director of the Teacher Education Department at Manhattanville College, has authored many textbooks and articles in professional journals, and has lectured at national and international conferences. As visiting professor at Teachers College Columbia University she ran the Intergenerational Literacy Program in Harlem, NY.

Joyce is the mother of two, the grandmother of three, and the great grandmother of one. She knows about needing a nap.

Both authors are members of the National League of American Pen Women and the International Reading Association.

Other Publications

More by Marie Z. Amoruso

Reading and Learning Disabilities (co-authored with J. French & N. Ellsworth)
K-12 English Language Arts Curriculum (NYS Dept. of Education - UFSD Irvington, NY)
Academic Intervention Services Program (K-12 Reading/Writing/Math Expectations)
Decoding by Meaningful Word Parts (research study)
Planning the Day (NYC Board of Education PS 86, Bronx, NY)
Learning to Read (CD-ROM)

More by Joyce N. French

Reading and Study Skills in the Secondary School (Garland Publishing, Inc)
Adult Literacy: A Source Book and Guide (Garland Publishing, Inc)
Teaching Thinking Skills: Theory and Practice (Garland Publishing, Inc)
Reading and Learning Disabilities: Research and Practice (Garland Publishing, Inc)